calm

calm

Steve Barnett

Andrews McMeel
Publishing

Kansas City

calm

06 07 08 09 10 WKT 10 9 8 7 6 5 4 3 2 1

ISBN-13: 978-0-7407-5667-2
ISBN-10: 0-7407-5667-2

Library of Congress Control Number: 2005932597

Composition by Kelly & Company, Lee's Summit, Missouri

ATTENTION: SCHOOLS AND BUSINESSES
Andrews McMeel books are available at quantity discounts with bulk purchase for educational, business, or sales promotional use. For information, please write to: Special Sales Department, Andrews McMeel Publishing, 4520 Main Street, Kansas City, Missouri 64111.

calm

The images and words that follow have been selected to bring together a world of serenity and calm. By *looking* into the images and *listening* to the words, you can discover a still and quiet place beyond the irritations and stresses of daily life. And in this place you may discover a perspective on life, draw some comfort, and find your center once again.

harmony

Here is the beauty of nature and expressions of meaning beyond the clamor of the world. Contemplate, and look beyond your cares.

tranquillity

Here is purpose and a sense of what matters and what does not. Here is a simplicity by which you can perhaps connect to the bigger picture, and in this way understand the place of those things that upset our equilibrium, and so regain our calm center. A source of strength.

relax

Let go for awhile, take a walk, sit outside at night. Sit in the sun, look up at the sky and clouds.

meditate

"Never be in a hurry; do everything quietly and in a calm spirit. Do not lose your inner peace for anything whatsoever, even if your whole world seems upset."
—Saint Francis de Sales

calm

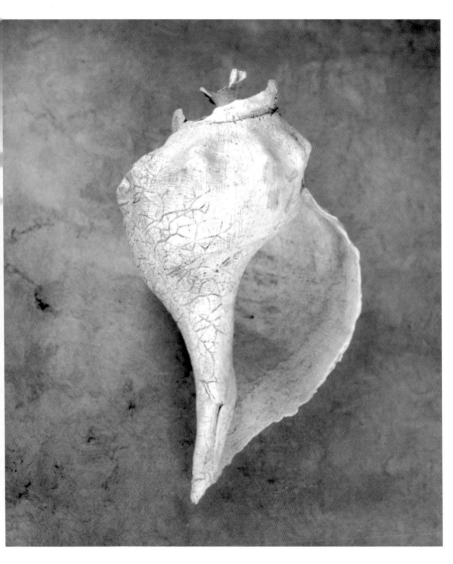

relax

summer

still

silence

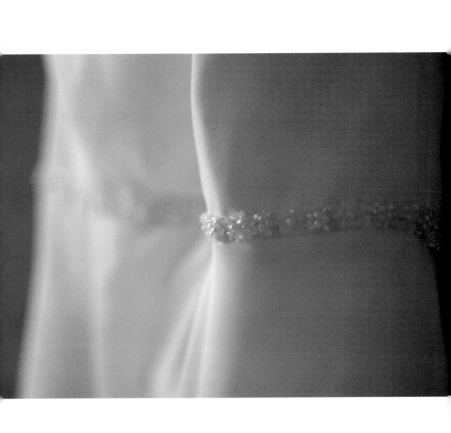

peace

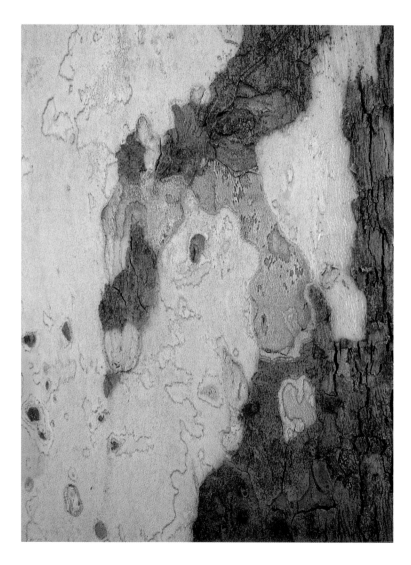

harmony

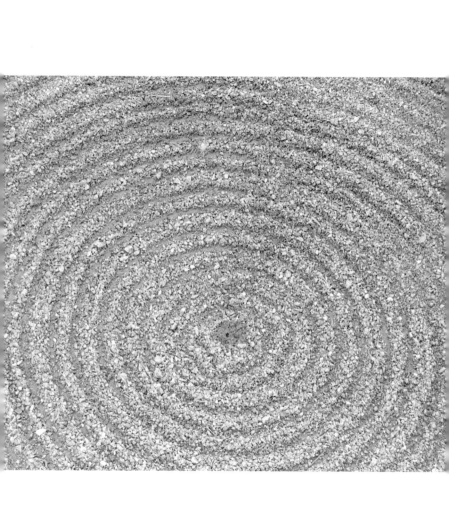

grace

"He said the pleasantest manner of spending a hot July day was lying from morning till evening on a bank of heath in the middle of the moors, with the bees humming dreamily about among the bloom, and the larks singing high up overhead, and the blue sky and the bright sun shining steadily and cloudlessly. That was his most perfect idea of heaven's happiness."

—EMILY BRONTË, *Wuthering Heights*

"*Everybody* should have his personal sounds to listen for—sounds that will make him exhilarated and alive or quiet and calm."

—ANDRE KOSTELANETZ

"The synthesis of pure, calming food is breathing pure air, listening to good sounds, looking at good sights, and touching pure objects."

—SRI SATHYA SAI BABA

"*Beautiful* music is the art of the prophets that can calm the agitations of the soul; it is one of the most magnificent and delightful presents God has given us."

—MARTIN LUTHER

"The whole secret of existence is to have no fear. Never fear what will become of you; depend on no one. Only the moment you reject all help are you freed."

—BUDDHA

"Nothing can bring you peace but yourself; nothing, but the triumph of principles."

—RALPH WALDO EMERSON

"He who is of calm and happy nature will hardly feel the pressure of age, but to him who is of an opposite disposition, youth and age are equally a burden."

—PLATO

"As you simplify your life, the laws of the universe will be simpler; solitude will not be solitude, poverty will not be poverty, nor weakness."

—HENRY DAVID THOREAU

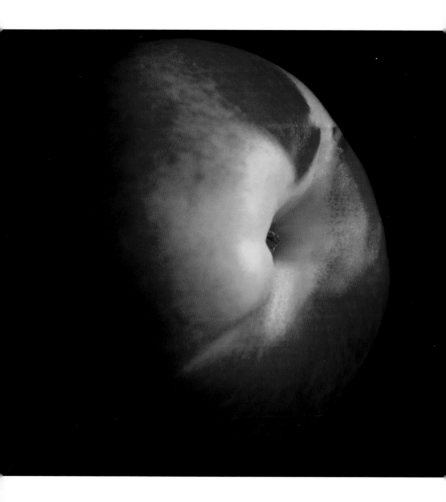

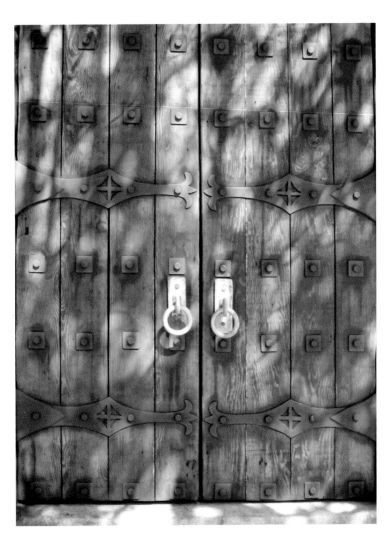

"*Be* so strong that nothing can disturb your peace of mind."

—CHRISTIAN LARSON

"*If* a man's mind becomes pure, his surroundings will also become pure."

—BUDDHA

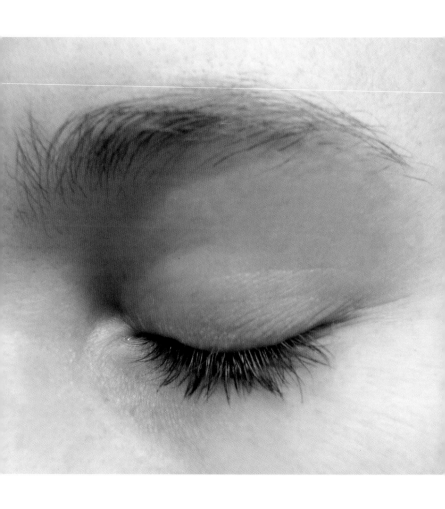

"What I dream of is an art of balance, of purity and serenity devoid of troubling or depressing subject matter—a soothing, calming influence on the mind, rather like a good armchair which provides relaxation from physical fatigue."

—HENRI MATISSE

"Man should forget his anger before he lies down to sleep."

—THOMAS DE QUINCEY

"The secret of success is to be in harmony with existence, to be always calm, to let each wave of life wash us a little farther up the shore."

—Cyril Connolly

"Inward calm cannot be maintained unless physical strength is constantly and intelligently replenished."

—BUDDHA

"Do not lose your inward peace for anything whatsoever, even if your whole world seems upset."

—Saint Francis de Sales

"Calmness is the cradle of power."

—JOSIAH GILBERT HOLLAND

"*Never* be in a hurry; do everything quietly and in a calm spirit."

—SAINT FRANCIS DE SALES

"Always direct your thoughts to those truths that will give you confidence, hope, joy, love, thanksgiving, and turn away your mind from those that inspire you with fear, sadness, depression."

—BERTRAND WILBERTFORCE

"To have a quiet mind is to possess one's mind wholly; to have a calm spirit is to possess one's self."

—HAMILTON WRIGHT MABIE

"Dwell as near as possible to the channel in which your life flows."

—HENRY DAVID THOREAU

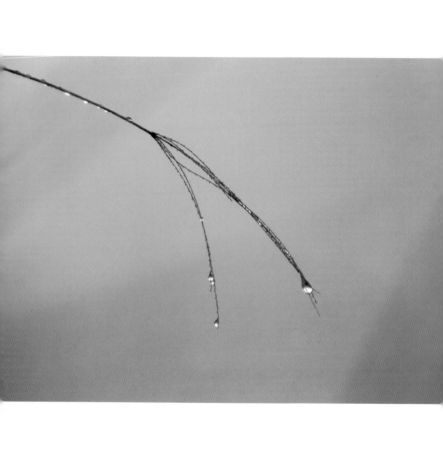

serene

tranquil

stillness

lull

meditate

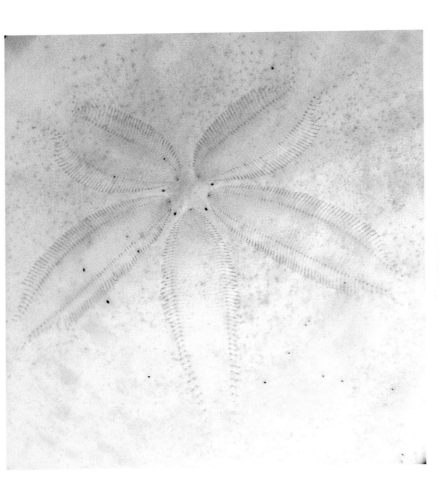

soothe

dream

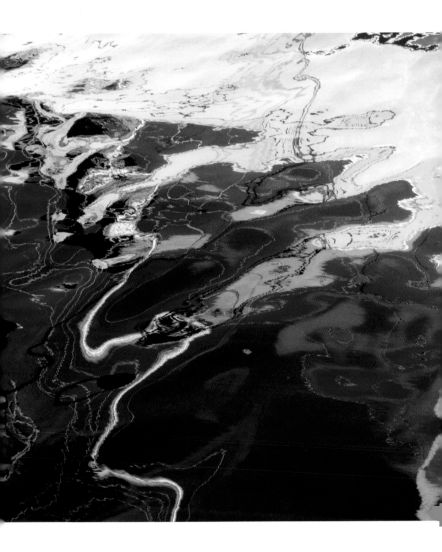

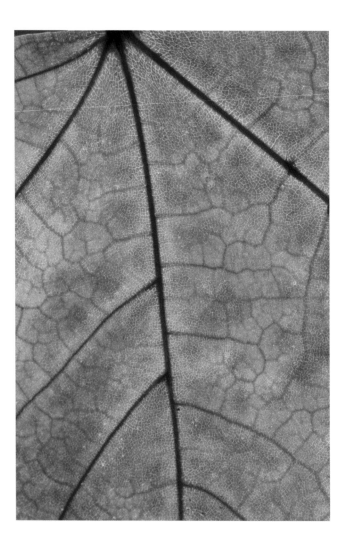

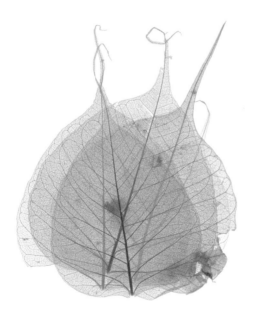

quiet

calm